To R
good times

Retirement
Plan

Congratulations on your Retirement!

Use this journal to record your retirement adventures, bucket list ideas, things to accomplish, places to visit or just for everyday notes.

Wishing you long years of adventure, fun and

we live in deeds, not years: in thoughts, not breaths.

- PJ Bailey

We know what we are now, but not what
we may become.

- Shakespeare

Do not take life too seriously – you will
never get out of it alive.

- Elbert Hubbard

Life is not a problem to be solved,
but a reality to be experienced.

- PJ Bailey

Express Gratitude Daily.

Life is a song - sing it. Life is a game - play it. Life is a challenge - meet it. Life is a dream - realize it. Life is a sacrifice - offer it. Life is love - enjoy it.

- Sai Baba

Thousands of candles can be lighted from a
single candle, and the life of the candle will
not be shortened. Happiness never decreases by
being shared.

- Buddha

Good health and good sense are two of
life's greatest blessings.

- Thomas Jefferson

It is neither wealth nor splendor; but tranquility and occupation which give you happiness.

- Thomas Jefferson

There are two great days in a person's life - the day we are born and the day we discover why.

- W.S. Blatchley

Be happy for this moment. This moment is your life.

- Omar Khayyam

Each of us is limitless—each of us with
his or her right upon the earth.

- Walt Whitman

No one can have a peaceful life who
thinks too much about lengthening it.

- Seneca

Keep your face to the sunshine and the
shadows will fall behind you.

- Walt Whitman

Good friends, good books and a sleepy
conscience; this is the ideal life.

- Mark Twain

No act of kindness, no matter how small, is ever wasted.

- Aesop

Made in the USA
Columbia, SC
12 April 2021